COOL ODOR DECODERS

Fun Science Projects about Smells

Esther Beck

ABDO
Publishing Company

TO ADULT HELPERS

You're invited to assist an up-and-coming scientist! And it will pay off in many ways. Your children can develop new skills, gain confidence, and do some interesting projects while learning about science. What's more, it's going to be a lot of fun!

These projects are designed to let children work independently as much as possible. Encourage them to do whatever they are able to do on their own. Also encourage them to try the variations when supplied and to keep a science journal. Encourage children to think like real scientists.

Before getting started, set some ground rules about using the materials and ingredients. Most important, adult supervision is a must whenever a child uses the stove, chemicals, or dry ice.

So put on your lab coats and stand by. Let your young scientists take the lead. Watch and learn. Praise their efforts. Enjoy the scientific adventure!

VISIT US AT WWW.ABDOPUBLISHING.COM

Published by ABDO Publishing Company, 8000 West 78th Street, Edina, Minnesota 55439. Copyright © 2008 by Abdo Consulting Group, Inc. International copyrights reserved in all countries. No part of this book may be reproduced in any form without written permission from the publisher. The Checkerboard Library™ is a trademark and logo of ABDO Publishing Company.

Printed in the United States.

Design and Production: Mighty Media, Inc.
Art Direction: Kelly Doudna
Photo Credits: Kelly Doudna, AbleStock, iStockphoto/Maartje van Caspel, JupiterImages Corporation, Photodisc, Shutterstock
Series Editor: Pam Price
Consultant: Scott Devens

The following manufacturers/names appearing in this book are trademarks: Archer Farms, Chicken of the Sea, French's, Jerzees, Knox, Liberty Gold, McCormick, Mezzetta, Target, TruTemp, Sharpie, Skippy

Library of Congress Cataloging-in-Publication Data
Beck, Esther.
  Cool odor decoders : fun science projects about smells / Esther Beck.
      p. cm. -- (Cool science)
  Includes index.
  ISBN 978-1-59928-909-0
  1. Science projects--Juvenile literature. 2. Odors--Juvenile literature.
  3. Science--Experiments--Juvenile literature. I. Title.

Q182.3.B4354 2008
507.8--dc22

                                                    2007005989

Contents

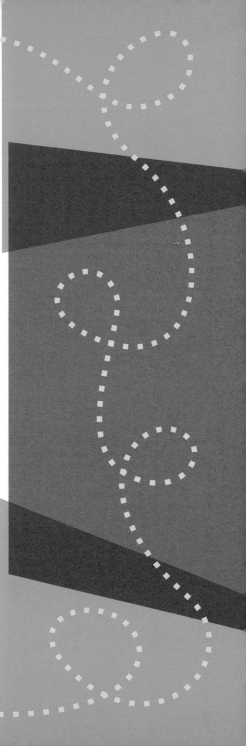

Science Is Cool

Welcome to the cool world of science! Before we get started, let's put on our thinking caps. What do the following things have in common?

- bubbles in soda pop
  - helium balloons that stay up in the air
    - sounds you hear through the headphones of your music player
      - a telescope that makes the faraway moon and stars appear closer
      - choosing your right or left eye to look through a camera viewfinder
  - your ability to balance on one foot

Did you guess that what they have in common is science? That's right, science! When you think of science, maybe you picture someone in a laboratory wearing a long white coat. Perhaps you imagine a scientist hunched over bubbling beakers and test tubes. But science is so much more. Let's take another look.

Soda pop doesn't develop bubbles until you open the container. That's because of a science called chemistry. Chemistry also explains why helium inside a balloon causes it to rise through the air.

You listen to your favorite song through the headphones attached to your music player. You look at the moon and stars through a telescope. Both activities are possible because of a science called physics. Did you know that eyeglasses improve your vision for the same reason telescopes work?

You tend to use the same eye each time you look through a camera viewfinder. You might find it challenging to balance on one foot. The science of biology helps explain why. Did you know it's related to the reason most people use only their left hand or right hand to write?

Broadly defined, science is the study of everything around us. Scientists use experiments and research to figure out how things work and relate to each other. The cool thing about science is that anyone can do it. You don't have to be a scientist in a laboratory to do science. You can do experiments with everyday things!

The Cool Science series introduces you to the world of science. Each book in this series will guide you through several simple experiments and projects with a common theme. The experiments use easy-to-find materials. Step-by-step instructions and photographs help guide your work.

The Scientific Method

Scientists have a special way of working. It is called the scientific method. The scientific method is a series of steps that a scientist follows when trying to learn something. Following the steps makes it more likely that the information you discover will be reliable.

The scientific method is described on the next page. Follow all of the steps. These steps will help you learn the best information possible. And then you can draw an accurate conclusion about what happened. You will even write notes in your own science journal, just like real scientists do!

EVEN COOLER!
Check out sections like this one throughout the book. Here you'll find instructions for variations on the project. It might be a suggestion for a different way to do the project. Or it might be a similar project that uses slightly different materials. Either way, it will make your science project even cooler!

1. Observe

Simply pay attention to something. This is called observing. A good way to prepare for the next step is to make up a what, why, or how question about what you observe. For example, let's say you observe that when you open a bottle of soda pop and pour it into a glass, it gets bubbly. Your question could be, How do bubbles get into soda?

2. Hypothesize

Think of a statement that could explain what you have observed. This statement is called a hypothesis. You might remember that you also saw bubbles in your milk when you blew into it with a straw. So your hypothesis might be, I think somebody used a straw to blow into the soda before the bottle was sealed.

3. Test

Test your hypothesis. You do this by conducting an experiment. To test your hypothesis about how bubbles get into soda, you might mix up a recipe, blow into the liquid with a straw, quickly close the container, and then open it back up.

4. Conclude

Draw a conclusion. When you do this, you tie together everything that happened in the previous steps. You report whether the result of the experiment was what you hypothesized. Perhaps there were no bubbles in your soda pop recipe when you reopened the container. You would conclude that blowing through a straw is not how fizz gets into liquids.

Write It Down

A large part of what makes science science is observation. You should observe what happens as you work through an experiment. Scientists observe everything and write notes about it in journals. You can keep a science journal too. All you need is a notebook and a pencil.

At the beginning of each activity in this book, there is a section called "Think Like a Scientist." It contains suggestions about what to record in your science journal. You can predict what you think will happen. You can write down what did happen. And you can draw a conclusion, especially if what really happened is different from what you predicted.

As you do experiments, record things in your journal. You will be working just like a real scientist!

THINK LIKE A SCIENTIST!
Look for a box like this one on the first page of each project. It will give you ideas about what to write in your science journal before, during, and after your experiments. There may be questions about the project. There may be a suggestion about how to look at the project in a different way. Your science journal is the place to keep track of everything!

EVEN COOLER!
You can record more than just words in your journal. You can sketch pictures and make charts. If you have a camera, you can even add photos to your journal!

Safe Science

Good scientists practice safe science. Here are some important things to remember.

- Check with an adult before you begin any project. Sometimes you'll need an adult to buy materials or help you handle them for a while. For some projects, an adult will need to help you the whole time. The instructions will say when an adult should assist you.

- Ask for help if you're unsure about how to do something.

- If you or someone else is hurt, tell an adult immediately.

- Read the list of things you'll need. Gather everything before you begin working on a project.

- Don't taste, eat, or drink any of the materials or the results unless the directions say that you can.

- Use protective gear. Scientists wear safety goggles to protect their eyes. They wear gloves to protect their hands from chemicals and possible burns. They wear aprons or lab coats to protect their clothing.

- Clean up when you are finished. That includes putting away materials and washing containers, work surfaces, and your hands.

9

Cool Odor Decoders

Most people smell things every day without even thinking about it. But there's real science behind our sense of smell.

When we smell, we take in chemicals called odorants that are dissolved in the air. Receptor cells in our noses receive these odorants, or odors. Then the **olfactory** part of the brain processes information about the smells. It tells us that something smells good! And it tells us that something smells nasty!

Human beings have about 40 million such receptor cells. With these receptors, we can recognize up to 10,000 odors. Some people can smell better than others.

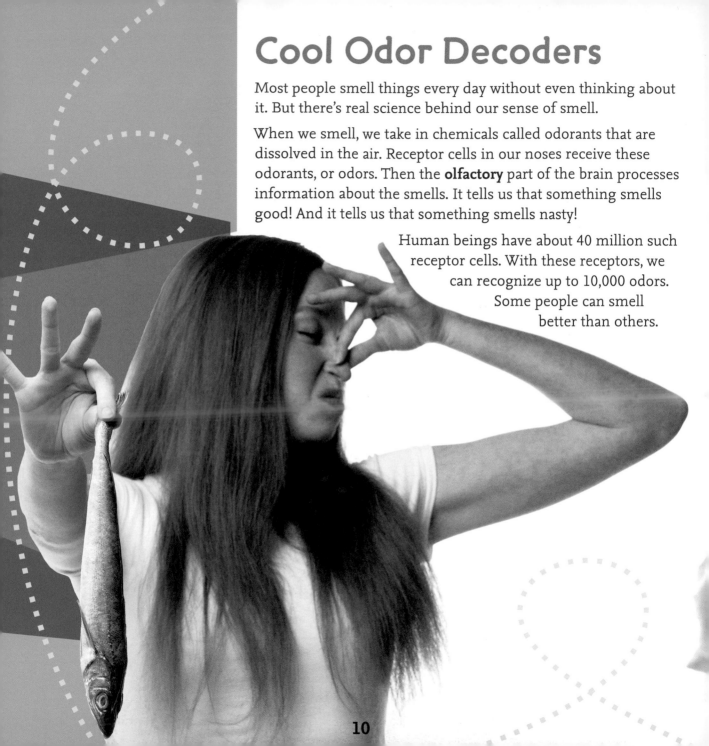

For example, women are usually better smellers than men. And as we age, we all lose some sense of smell.

Some people can't smell at all. They have a disorder called anosmia. This condition sounds harmless, but it can be dangerous. People who have it can't smell smoke, gas leaks, or spoiled food.

They also don't experience memories triggered by smells. Perhaps the smell of warm banana bread makes you think of your aunt. Or maybe the smell of spring rain brings to mind wearing your favorite yellow raincoat. Here's why. The parts of the brain used to process smell and remember events are near each other.

In general, no two people **perceive** odors the same way. The activities in this book will put your nose to the test. The odors range from the super smelly to the **sublime**. Think of them as fun "smelling tests" that don't require studying! So **recruit** some buddies, gather an odorant or two, and get a whiff of that!

Materials

You can probably find these supplies around the house.

cotton swabs   rubbing alcohol   small, clean jars with lids   marker

thermometer (optional)   matching paper cups   aluminum foil   scissors

clock   rubber gloves   plastic freezer bags (gallon size)   pine needles

AT THE GROCERY STORE
You can find these supplies at a grocery store.

cinnamon sticks

vanilla extract

lemon peel

freezer pop

garlic clove

onion

can of tuna

whole cloves

lemons

mustard

peanut butter

peppermint

unflavored gelatin

AT THE DISCOUNT STORE
You can find these supplies at a discount store.

MISCELLANEOUS
You can find these at
a science supply store.

several different colors
of balloons

matching kid-size
T-shirts

matching adult-size
T-shirts

petri dishes

13

Host a Stink Fest!

Join forces with your friends to do the smelliest science experiment ever! All you need are a few household items and some odor **ingenuity**. How much stink can you make? How much stink can you take?

MATERIALS

several different colors of balloons

cotton swabs

garlic clove

onion

can of tuna

other smelly items, use your imagination!

CHEMISTRY

THINK LIKE A SCIENTIST!
Rate the intensity of each odor you created. Use this scale, called the Likert Scale, and record your findings in your science journal. Compare your ratings to a friend's. Do your ratings differ?

0 no odor

1 weak odor

2 noticeable odor

3 strong odor

4 extreme odor

1 Crush the garlic clove and rub the cotton swab in its juice.

2 Rub the swab inside a balloon, but not too close to the open end.

3 Blow up the balloon and tie a knot in its end.

4 In your science journal, note which color of balloon contains the garlic.

5 Now repeat the process with the other stinky stuff. Put each item in a different balloon. Be sure to track which substance is in which balloon!

6 Smell the outside of each balloon. What do you smell? Is there much difference between them?

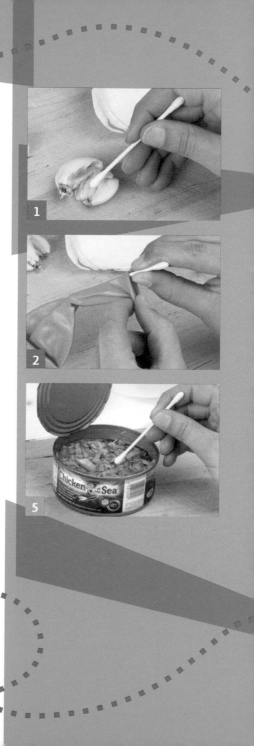

The Science behind the Fun

The balloons have tiny holes called pores in them. These pores don't allow air to escape, so the balloons stay inflated. But the pores do allow some smaller garlic, onion, and tuna molecules through. In science-speak, this movement of a dissolved substance through a membrane is called osmosis. Osmosis is what allows the odor molecules through the balloon but not the air.

☆✦ EVEN COOLER!

Turn up the heat and extend the experiment. Place each balloon near, but not touching, an **incandescent** light bulb. What do you notice about the odor the balloon gives off? When the balloon comes back to room temperature, place it in a freezer for about five to ten seconds. Take another whiff. Do you notice any change?

Science at Work

Osmosis is how water travels from one cell to another. In biology class you will study cells and learn more about osmosis.

How Sweet It Is

MATERIALS
rubbing alcohol
small, clean jars
with lids
whole cloves
cinnamon sticks
vanilla extract
lemon peel
cotton swabs

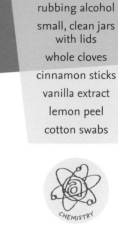
CHEMISTRY

Not everything that's smelly is stinky. In this activity, you'll make your own **signature** perfume. Sweet!

THINK LIKE A SCIENTIST!
Record your perfume recipes in your science journal as you work. That way you'll be able to make more of the ones you really like.

17

1 Place about two ounces (60 ml) of rubbing alcohol in a jar.

2 Add 12 cloves, several small pieces of cinnamon stick, one teaspoon (5 ml) of vanilla extract, and some lemon peel to the alcohol.

3 Put the lid on the jar and let it sit for about a week.

4 Place a small amount of the perfume on the inside of your wrist. Wait for it to evaporate. How does it smell?

5 Repeat the activity, trying different perfume recipes, until you create the scent you like best!

The Science behind the Fun

Here's the science secret behind perfume. As perfume evaporates, its vapor enters the nose. The alcohol evaporates first, leaving behind the good-smelling oils. These oils remain on the skin and create an attractive scent.

EVEN COOLER!

Here's an even easier recipe for perfume.

MATERIALS

flower petals (ask the gardener before picking flowers or buy flowers from a florist)

water
small bowl
spoon

tissue paper
funnel
empty jar or plastic spray bottle

1. Break the flower petals into small pieces. Place the petal pieces in the small bowl.

2. Add a small amount of water. Now mash the petals with the back of the spoon.

3. Let the mixture sit for 15 minutes.

4. Place the tissue paper in the funnel to create a filter.

5. Pour the mixture into the filter. Let the water drip into the empty jar or spray bottle.

6. Use the perfume on the inside of your wrist. Or, use it to freshen the air. Be sure to keep it away from your eyes when you spray it!

7. Make your own designer perfume! Combine the scented water from different kinds of flowers.

Science at Work

In the perfume industry, the person who mixes ingredients to make fine perfumes is called the nose. The nose is part chemist and part artist. This person combines oils and chemicals to create the perfect scent. A talented nose's sniffer is trained to recognize even the most **subtle** smells!

Temp Test

MATERIALS

2 freezer pops

2 paper cups

freezer

thermometer (optional)

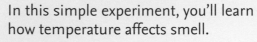

In this simple experiment, you'll learn how temperature affects smell.

CHEMISTRY

THINK LIKE A SCIENTIST!
Are you feeling really ambitious? Add some data collection to the mix. Take the temperature of the freezer pop every three minutes as it's melting. Smell the freezer pop each time you take the temperature. Make a table and record your data in your science journal.

	Temp.	How does it smell?
3 minutes		
6 minutes		
9 minutes		
12 minutes		
15 minutes		

1 Place one freezer pop in each cup. If you have a double freezer pop, split it in two first and put one half in each cup.

2 Put one cup in the freezer.

3 Set the other cup on a table until the freezer pop melts. It will take about 15 minutes.

4 Remove the first freezer pop from the freezer.

5 Now smell each freezer pop. What do you notice?

The Science behind the Fun

When a material warms up, its particles may vaporize. These particles then launch into your nose. There, they orbit by your odor receptors.

Science at Work

Here's an everyday example of how smelling something warm gets your attention. When dinner is ready, it's not the cold, crisp salad that draws you to the table. It's the warm food that comes calling your nose!

Smelling Test

TIME: ABOUT 20 MINUTES

How good is your snout?
See what your nose knows
with this matching activity.

MATERIALS

items that smell,
such as
lemons
onions
pine needles
mustard
tuna
peppermint

paper cups that
all look alike

aluminum foil

scissors

CHEMISTRY

THINK LIKE A SCIENTIST!

* Try this activity with friends. Use your science journal to track how each person does. Could you all identify the same smells?

* Try this activity the next time you have a cold. Compare how you do with notes from when you were healthy. Is there a difference? What do you think is happening?

* Keep a list of smelly items to use the next time you try this activity.

1 Divide each smelly item into two portions. Put each portion in a separate paper cup.

2 Cover the cups with aluminum foil. Use the scissors to make a small hole in the top of each one.

3 Mix up the cups.

4 Now try to match the pairs of cups that contain the same item. Place your guesses beside each other and keep working!

5 Remove the aluminum foil covers to check your guesses.

The Science behind the Fun

Here's an interesting bit of nose science. After we've smelled an odor for a few minutes, we can't smell it anymore. That's because our receptor cells are tired and need a rest. But we can still smell other odors by using other receptor cells. This activity alternates between odors and calls on different receptor cells. So your nose should be in good shape for it!

Science at Work

Being able to identify smells is good fun. And it's important for safety reasons as well. Our noses help us know when food has turned bad, when a pan is burning on the stovetop, or if there's a gas leak in the house. Can you think of other examples of when noses could save the day? Jot your ideas in your science journal.

Bodyworks

TIME: ABOUT 15 MINUTES, THEN 5 DAYS

MATERIALS
3 petri dishes
unflavored gelatin
water
clock
cotton swabs
rubber gloves

Did you know that it's actually **bacteria** that cause body odor? In this investigation, you'll take **microbe** samples from your feet, underarms, and mouth. Then you'll see which has the most **potential** for stink!

BIOLOGY

ARMPIT

TOES

THINK LIKE A SCIENTIST!
Check the petri dishes every day as you are growing the cultures. Write your observations in your science journal. Draw pictures of the bacteria if you like! Can you tell anything about the bacteria from their color or shape? Do some research to try to identify the bacteria.

This activity requires an adult assistant. Find a good **recruit** before starting.

1 Have an adult help you prepare the gelatin. Follow the directions on the package. Let the gelatin cool for several minutes before handling it.

2 Pour gelatin into each of the petri dishes. Let the gelatin set up in the dishes for about four hours.

3 Brush inside your mouth and along your tongue with a cotton swab.

4 Then brush the swab into the gelatin in one of the dishes. Label the outside of the petri dish.

5 Use new cotton swabs to repeat steps 3 and 4, taking bacteria samples from under your arms and between your toes. Label each petri dish.

6 Place the dishes in a dark, cool area for five days.

7 Compare the dishes to see which grew the most bacteria. You will be able to see the bacteria. But you won't be able to smell it through the gelatin.

Cleanup Time!

Be sure to wear gloves. Do not handle the **bacteria** directly as it can cause disease.

1. Have an adult help you boil some water.

2. Place the petri dishes in the sink. Ask your helper to pour the hot water into the petri dishes. He or she should pour until the gelatin becomes liquid. Then pour the gelatin down the sink. Run plenty of water to flush the gelatin through the drain.

3. Throw the petri dishes away.

The Science behind the Fun

Bacteria on the human body may sound like a problem, but mostly it's not. Some bacteria are actually good for us. Some are harmless. And only certain kinds can make us sick.

Many bacteria cells live on our skin and in our digestive **tracts**. Scientists estimate that there are up to 1,000 different kinds of bacteria in a body. In fact, there are ten times more bacteria cells than human cells in our bodies!

Science at Work

Antibacterial soaps and wipes were originally designed for hospital use. These days, they are found in many homes too. Scientists worry that overusing these products may cause bacteria to become resistant to them. And they worry that our immune systems may not work as well as a result. Because of this possibility, many people choose regular soap instead of antibacterial soap.

All In the Family

TIME: ABOUT 5 DAYS

MATERIALS

5 matching kid-size T-shirts

5 matching adult-size T-shirts

10 plastic freezer bags (gallon size)

marker

5 friends

5 parents of the friends

Can you identify your parent's scent? Can he or she identify yours? Find out with this experiment. It puts our ability to smell pheromones to the test.

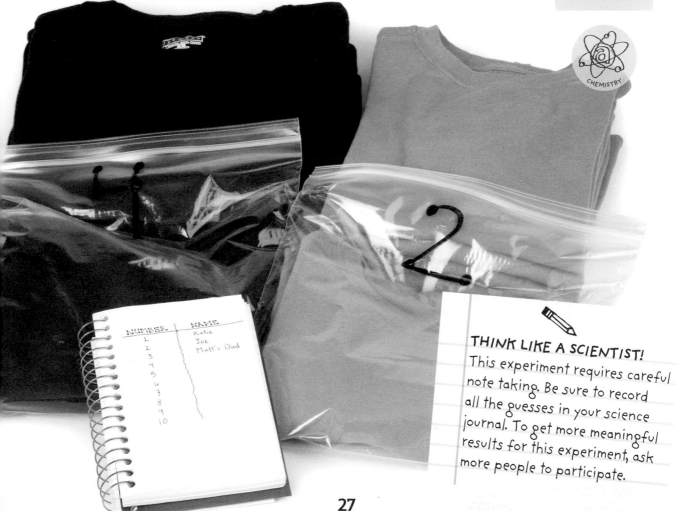

CHEMISTRY

NUMBER | NAME
1 | Katie
2 | Joe
3 | Matt's Dad
4 |
5 |
6 |
7 |
8 |
9 |
10 |

THINK LIKE A SCIENTIST!

This experiment requires careful note taking. Be sure to record all the guesses in your science journal. To get more meaningful results for this experiment, ask more people to participate.

27

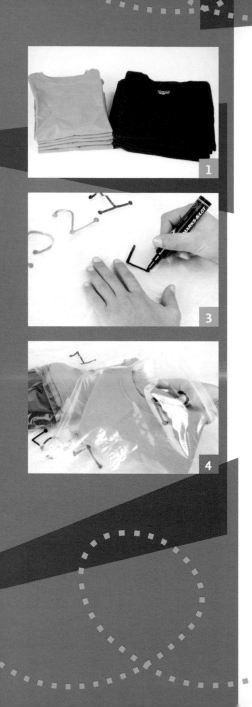

1 Give one T-shirt to each participant in the experiment.

2 Have each participant sleep in a shirt for five nights and return it to you unwashed.

3 Label ten plastic bags with the numbers 1 through 10.

4 Place each shirt in its own plastic bag. Keep a record in your journal of whose shirt is in each bag.

5 Hold a smell-in. Invite each parent to smell the five kids' T-shirts. Ask the parents if they can determine which shirt belongs to their child. Keep track of their answers.

6 Then have each kid smell the five adults' T-shirts. See if they can determine which shirts belong to their parents. Keep track of their answers.

The Science behind the Fun

Pheromones are body chemicals. Animals use them to affect how other animals behave. Pheromones also give each person a special smell.

EVEN COOLER!
Expand this experiment to see how and if the results change. For example, compare the results of boys to girls or moms to dads. Or see how the results change when kids of different ages are tested. Do you think you can smell better than a three-year-old?
Give it a try!

Science at Work

You see pheromones at work when dogs sniff each other. Other mammals and reptiles do the same thing. Scientists have even found that breast-fed babies can identify their mothers just a few days after birth! Now that's smart!

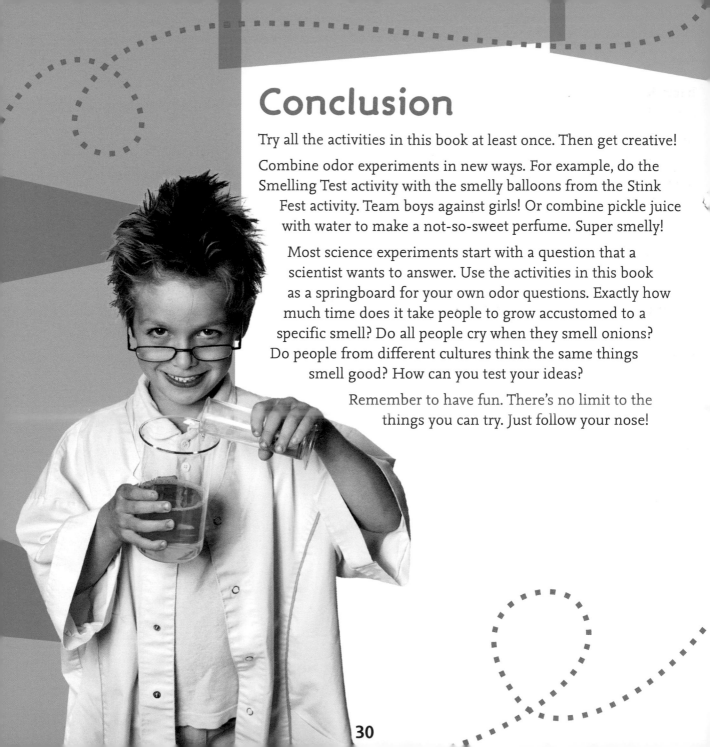

Conclusion

Try all the activities in this book at least once. Then get creative!

Combine odor experiments in new ways. For example, do the Smelling Test activity with the smelly balloons from the Stink Fest activity. Team boys against girls! Or combine pickle juice with water to make a not-so-sweet perfume. Super smelly!

Most science experiments start with a question that a scientist wants to answer. Use the activities in this book as a springboard for your own odor questions. Exactly how much time does it take people to grow accustomed to a specific smell? Do all people cry when they smell onions? Do people from different cultures think the same things smell good? How can you test your ideas?

Remember to have fun. There's no limit to the things you can try. Just follow your nose!

Glossary

bacteria – tiny, one-celled organisms that can be seen only through a microscope.

incandescent – an electric light bulb that produces light when a fine wire is heated by electrical current.

ingenuity – skill or cleverness when designing or planning something.

microbe – a microorganism or germ.

olfactory – of or relating to the sense of smell.

perceive – to use the senses to become aware of something.

potential – capable of being or becoming. Something that is possible, but not actual.

recruit – to get someone to join a group. A person who is recruited is also called a recruit.

signature – a characteristic that identifies something as being unique, or one of a kind.

sublime – inspiring awe because of its beauty or excellence.

subtle – so slight that it is hard to detect or identify.

tract – a system of body parts that work together to perform a function.

WEB SITES

To learn more about odors and smelling, visit ABDO Publishing Company on the World Wide Web at **www.abdopublishing. com.** Web sites about odors and smelling are featured on our Book Links page. These links are routinely monitored and updated to provide the most current information available.

Index